CAN YOU COUNT TO A GOOGOL?

Robert E. Wells

Albert Whitman & Company · Morton Grove, Illinois

For my nieces Susannah and Anna
and my nephews, John, Nathaniel, Brady, and Austin.
May the new millennium bring you googols of blessings!

Library of Congress Cataloging-in-Publication Data

Wells, Robert E.
Can you count to a googol? / written and
illustrated by Robert E. Wells.
p.   cm.
Summary: Introduces the concepts of very large numbers,
up to a googol, and multiples of ten.
ISBN 0-8075-1060-2
ISBN 0-8075-1061-0 (pbk.)
1. Decimal system—Juvenile literature. 2. Multiplication—
Juvenile literature. [1. Decimal system. 2. Multiplication.]
I. Title.
QA141.35.W45   2000   98-49759
513.5'5—dc21   CIP
                                             AC

Hand-lettering by Robert E. Wells.
The illustration media are pen and acrylic.
Design by Susan B. Cohn.

Because this is a book about counting,
the term *number,* when used in this book,
refers to COUNTING NUMBERS. Counting
numbers are whole numbers beginning
with 1 and continuing forever.

Also by Robert E. Wells
Is a Blue Whale the Biggest Thing There Is?
What's Smaller Than a Pygmy Shrew?
How Do You Lift a Lion?
What's Faster Than a Speeding Cheetah?

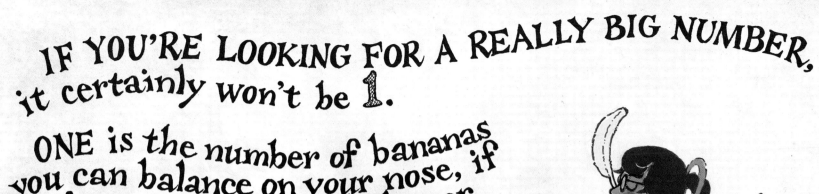

IF YOU'RE LOOKING FOR A REALLY BIG NUMBER, it certainly won't be 1.

ONE is the number of bananas you can balance on your nose, if you're a good banana balancer.

Put a ZERO after a 1, and it becomes 10. Whenever you put a ZERO after a number, it makes that number TEN times bigger.

TEN bananas would be a lot of bananas for a monkey to balance. But, of course, TEN is still very small.

10 × 10 is 100. Would you call ONE HUNDRED big? Well, no matter WHAT you call it, it's a lot of balanced bananas!

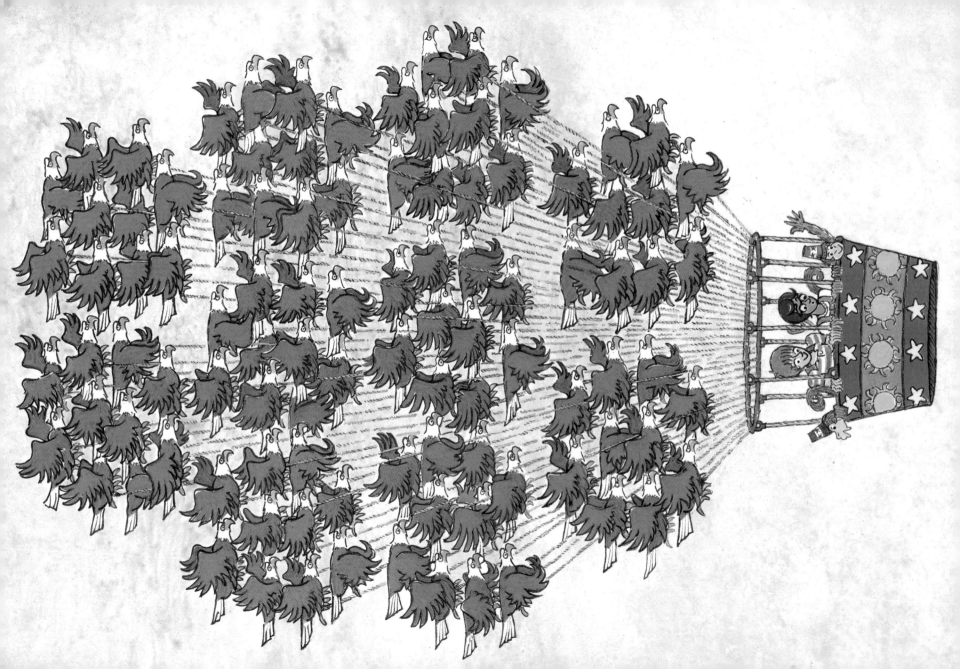

Perhaps 100 eagles could take you on a scenic ride high in the sky, if they were willing.

But, if you're searching for a really, REALLY big number, you still have a VERY long way to go!

10 × 100 is 1,000.

If ONE HUNDRED penguins each had TEN scoops of ice cream in a cone,

that would be ONE THOUSAND scoops of ice cream.
ONE THOUSAND is starting to get big.

But don't stop there!

ONE MILLION is 10 times bigger!
It looks like this: 1,000,000.

Sometimes, great distances are easier to measure in **MILLIONS**, such as

the distance between the earth and the sun.

← That's about 93 **MILLION** miles.

A MILLION is also useful for measuring long periods of time, such as the number of years that have passed since dinosaurs last roamed the earth. That's been about 65 MILLION years.

If you put ONE MILLION dollar bills in a money stacking and packing machine,

or, ONE HUNDRED MILLION dollars.

A BILLION is a MIGHTY big number. But, of course, TEN BILLION is TEN TIMES BIGGER!

It looks like this:
10,000,000,000.

Some stars in our Milky Way Galaxy are TEN BILLION years old.

Our SUN is a star. It's not that old yet, but someday it might be. It began to form about 5 BILLION years ago and will probably last at least 5 BILLION MORE years!

$10 \times 10{,}000{,}000{,}000$ is $100{,}000{,}000{,}000$, or, ONE HUNDRED BILLION. That's a TREMENDOUS number. But, as tremendous as it is, there are MORE than that many stars in our galaxy! Here are a few of them.

A TRILLION is an ENORMOUS, HUGE number!
It's TEN TIMES as big as a HUNDRED BILLION!
It looks like this:

1,000,000,000,000.

A TRILLION is just the right size
to help you think about the ENORMOUSLY
HUGE distances between stars in our galaxy.

It's about
25 TRILLION
miles

...from our sun to the next nearest star, PROXIMA CENTAURI

If you traveled at the speed of light, that trip would take over 4 years!

But numbers certainly don't stop at a TRILLION.

Here are three of the many numbers that are MUCH bigger.

Add 3 zeros to a TRILLION to get a QUADRILLION.

1,000,000,000,000,000

3 more zeros make a QUINTILLION.

1,000,000,000,000,000,000

How many zeros in an OCTILLION?

1,000,000,000,000,000,000,000,000,000

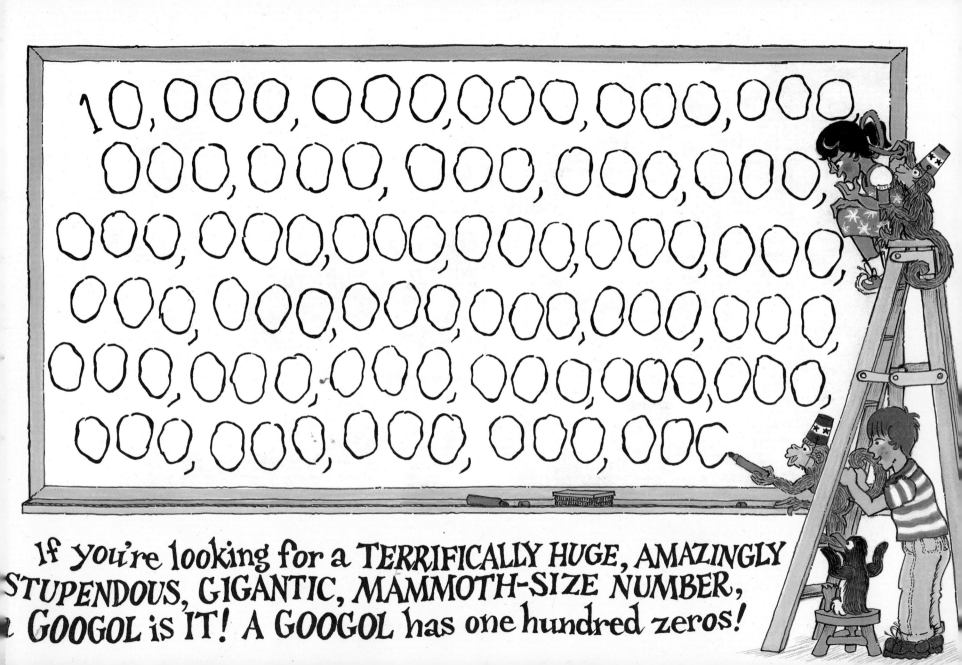

If you're looking for a TERRIFICALLY HUGE, AMAZINGLY STUPENDOUS, GIGANTIC, MAMMOTH-SIZE NUMBER, a GOOGOL is IT! A GOOGOL has one hundred zeros!

00,000,000,000,000,000,000,000,000,000,000,000,000,000

Did you ever wonder just how far FOREVER is?

HOW DO WE KNOW

...HOW BIG A STACK 1,000,000 DOLLAR BILLS WOULD MAKE?

 1,000 NEW, UNWRINKLED DOLLARS MAKE A STACK ABOUT 4 INCHES HIGH.

 10,000 MAKE A STACK ABOUT 40 INCHES HIGH.

...THE DISTANCE IN MILES FROM OUR SUN TO PROXIMA CENTAURI?

ASTRONOMERS KNOW HOW FAR LIGHT TRAVELS IN ONE YEAR— ALMOST 6 TRILLION MILES.

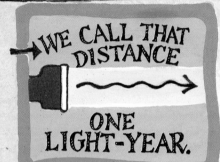 WE CALL THAT DISTANCE ONE LIGHT-YEAR.

IT'S ABOUT 4¼ LIGHT-YEARS FROM OUR SUN TO PROXIMA CENTAURI.

...THAT 100 EAGLES COULD REALLY TAKE YOU FOR A RIDE?

WE DON'T! A JOURNEY LIKE THAT CAN ONLY TAKE PLACE IN YOUR IMAGINATION!

BUT WE DO KNOW THIS:

 ONE EAGLE CAN CARRY A 3-POUND FISH.

1,000,000 WOULD BE 100 40-INCH STACKS. IN 10 ROWS OF 10, THEY'D MEASURE ABOUT

26 INCHES WIDE, 40 INCHES HIGH, AND 5 FEET LONG.

HOW LONG WOULD IT TAKE YOU TO SPEND $1,000,000?

OUR SUN

TO FIGURE OUT THE APPROXIMATE NUMBER OF MILES IN $4\frac{1}{4}$ LIGHT-YEARS, MULTIPLY $4\frac{1}{4}$ BY 6 TRILLION!

CAN YOU FIGURE OUT THE APPROXIMATE NUMBER OF MILES FROM OUR SUN TO PROXIMA CENTAURI?

PROXIMA CENTAURI

THAT MEANS 10 EAGLES COULD PROBABLY CARRY A 30-POUND FISH.

SO — COULD 100 EAGLES TAKE YOU FOR A RIDE — IF THEY WERE WILLING?

Yes, a Googol *Is* a Real Number!

One day in the late 1930s, Dr. Edward Kasner, an American mathematician, wrote down a number with 100 zeros. He didn't know what to call it, so he asked his nine-year-old nephew, Milton, to give it a name. Milton called it a GOOGOL— and so, on that day, a googol was born.

Over the years, the googol has captured the imagination of those who are fascinated by Very Big Numbers. But just how big *is* a googol?

With observations and calculations, astronomers can estimate how many atoms there are in all the billions of galaxies in the known universe, and in all the space between those galaxies. Some astronomers estimate that if you could count all those atoms, that number would be at least 10^{80}—or, a one followed by 80 zeros. But a googol, with 100 zeros, is ONE HUNDRED MILLION TRILLION TIMES BIGGER THAN THAT!

Of course, it's almost impossible to imagine such a big number. But isn't it kind of fun to try?

Wells, Robert E.
    Can you count to a googol?